FIRST
PHONE

FIRST PHONE

A CHILD'S GUIDE TO DIGITAL RESPONSIBILITY, SAFETY, AND ETIQUETTE

Catherine Pearlman, PhD, LCSW

ILLUSTRATIONS BY DAVE COVERLY

a TarcherPerigee book

tarcherperigee

an imprint of Penguin Random House LLC
penguinrandomhouse.com

Most TarcherPerigee books are available at special quantity discounts for bulk purchase for sales promotions, premiums, fund-raising, and educational needs. Special books or book excerpts also can be created to fit specific needs. For details, write: SpecialMarkets@penguinrandomhouse.com.

Library of Congress Cataloging-in-Publication Data

Names: Pearlman, Catherine, author.
Title: First phone: a child's guide to digital responsibility, safety, and etiquette / Catherine Pearlman, PhD, LCSW; illustrations by Dave Coverly.
Description: First edition. | New York: TarcherPerigee, an imprint of Penguin Random House LLC, [2022] | Audience: Ages 7. | Audience: Grades 2-3.
Identifiers: LCCN 2022005551 (print) | LCCN 2022005552 (ebook) | ISBN 9780593538333 (trade paperback) | ISBN 9780593538340 (epub)
Subjects: LCSH: Cell phones—Security measures—Juvenile literature. | Cell phone etiquette—Juvenile literature.
Classification: LCC TK6564.4.C45 P43 2022 (print) | LCC TK6564.4.C45 (ebook) | DDC 621.3845/6—dc23/eng/20220502
LC record available at https://lccn.loc.gov/2022005551
LC ebook record available at https://lccn.loc.gov/2022005552

Printed in the United States of America
1st Printing

Book design by Shannon Nicole Plunkett

TO ELLIE WERTHEIM AND ALISON CIMMET,
FOR KEEPING ME AFLOAT

AUTHOR'S NOTE

THIS BOOK FEATURES FIVE CHILDREN: MAX, SOFIA, JACK, MAYA, AND BENNI. These children are not actual kids I know. They are a mixture of many young friends of mine who helped advise me on this book. Their problems and their feelings represent the real lives of many children. But to keep identities private and to allow children to be honest, I have used composites of lots of children. I hope you enjoy meeting these five kids and find some commonalities with them. I have grown to love them.

CONTENTS

FIRST
PHONE

INTRODUCTION

CONGRATULATIONS ON GETTING A VERY EXCITING NEW SMARTPHONE. You are now the owner of one of the most powerful digital devices on earth. *Woohoo!*

Smartphones are minicomputers that can do just about anything a big computer can do but, in some ways, even more. Phones can fit in your pocket, making them handy. On your smartphone you can order a skateboard; video chat with family members around the world; log in to your classroom; play games; read a book; listen to music; learn how to make lasagna; take, edit, and share pictures.

Because smartphones are so powerful, they are also expensive. Keeping your phone safe and not losing it will be important.

Also, sometimes kids aren't prepared for all the responsibility that comes with the incredible power of a smartphone. That's why I wrote this book. I want to help you learn the ways to have fun using your digital device—but also how to stay safe.

Most kids know they want a phone, often because their friends and siblings have one. But once they get one, they can become overwhelmed with decisions, social situations, and setting appropriate limits. There are lots of lessons to learn to ensure safety for you and your friends. Some common questions that come up for kids when they receive their first phone are:

- What do I do if a new online friend I don't know asks for my address or personal information, like my birthday?

- Where should I keep my phone at night?

- What's safe to post online, and what should be avoided?

- When is the right time to join social media like TikTok and Instagram?

- What do I do if someone sends me an inappropriate picture or tries to bully me online?

- What do I do if I make a mistake?

In this book I will answer these questions and many more. Because I'm a grown-up, I have some young friends who will help with keeping it real. Throughout the pages that follow, they will share their experiences—the good ones, the bad ones, and the really embarrassing ones, too. That way, you can learn from what they've gone through.

Now, let me introduce you to . . . Sofia, Maya Jack, Benni, and Max!

"Hi. My name is Sofia. I'm nine years old, and I *love* anything with rainbows, unicorns, or sparkles. I like to bake, do art projects, and play with my dog, Rocko. I like math class because I'm good with numbers. But I really dislike reading because it's so hard for me. That's because I have a learning difference called dyslexia. My parents gave me a phone to help me keep in touch with my family who live across the country. I listen to a lot of audio books to help me read, and I like to have my phone in my pocket, too, if I walk to my friend Leah's house around the corner."

"My name is Max. I'm twelve years old, and I like to play *Mario Kart* and watch videos on TikTok. I use my phone a lot, but one important way is to control my diabetes. That's a disease that requires me to monitor my blood sugar. My phone alerts me when I need to adjust my medicine. It's kind of a lifesaver."

"My name is Jack. I enjoy playing video games and basketball, building robots, and trying new and exotic foods. My mom is in the military, so sometimes she works in another country. She gave me a phone to help us keep in touch. I'm eleven, but I got my phone when I was ten."

"My name is Benni, and I'm thirteen years old. My parents call me a social butterfly because I am friendly to everyone. I like to dance, sing, act, sew, and dress up. I was born a boy, but I dress like a girl. I often use my smartphone to contact my mom to pick me up after ballet. Mostly, I'm texting my friends. I love to stay in touch when we aren't at school."

"I'm Maya. I'm really into art, so I watch how-to videos on YouTube a lot. I also love American Girl and reading. I read just about anything I can find. My parents are divorced, which means they don't live together. They bought me a phone so it would be easy for me to contact the other parent when I'm not at their house. Oh, and I just turned twelve."

You may have heard grown-ups discussing the good and bad of smartphones for kids. There certainly are some concerns and dangers. Don't worry, we are going to go through all of that in this book. By the time you finish *First Phone*, you will know how to stay protected and make good decisions online. But first, let's focus on some of the fun stuff to do with your new smartphone.

Here are a few of our favorite ways to use a phone:

COMMUNICATION

Texting (**BENNI**: "That's my favorite thing.")

Email—send notes to your teacher or coach

Video calls to family far away (**SOFIA**: "I call my cousins on Sundays, and we talk for hours; also my grandpa does a video Spanish lesson every week.")

LEARNING

School apps like Canvas, Notability, and Quizlet (digital flash cards)

Khan Academy for math tutoring (**BENNI**: "I use Khan Academy whenever I don't understand something or when I want extra practice. It really helps.")

Reading apps (**SOFIA**: "I use one that reads all my assignments out loud. It helps me with reading.")

Language apps (**JACK**: "I use Duolingo to learn Spanish.")

Calculator

Google Maps

Audio books

CALENDARS AND REMINDERS

Reminders to feed the dog or call Grandma on her birthday

Make a schedule for chores and homework

Reminder for your allowance (Your parents may not always remember.)

(**MAYA**: "My parents fill out a Google Calendar for me so I know exactly which days I'm at my mom's house and which days I'm at my dad's. We all have access to it, so I can add in my after-school activities, too.")

BEING CREATIVE

Taking and editing pictures

Drawing

Listening to, creating, and editing music

Creating videos (**BENNI**: "I'm obsessed with making videos. I write scripts, and my friends act out the parts.")

GAMES

MAYA: "My favorites are Words With Friends and Mad Libs."

JACK: "I play lots of Minecraft and Roblox."

MAX: "I always play Pokémon GO."

BENNI: "My favorites are Scribblenauts and Monument Valley."

HEALTH

Headspace for Kids teaches mindfulness to improve focus, sleep, and relaxation. (**MAYA**: "I use mindfulness when I get nervous before trying something new.")

Fitness apps that count steps and offer yoga and other exercise activities (**SOFIA**: "I love to count my daily steps. My record is 9,321 steps.")

Diabetes trackers like Dexcom (**MAX**: "That's the one I use!")

How is it possible that one small device can do so much? It's really amazing.

One last thing before we move on. This book is written just for you, but at the end of the book, I'll include some short notes for the adults in your life. That way you can feel comfortable talking to them about what you are learning and then ask any questions as they come up.

OK, let's get started.

CHAPTER 1

WHO NEEDS RULES?

BACK WHEN MY SON, EMMETT, WAS IN THIRD GRADE, HE HAD A WONDERFUL TEACHER NAMED MRS. BOYS. If a student raised their hand to ask to go to the bathroom or to sharpen a pencil or to grab a book off the shelf, Mrs. Boys would respond with three magical words: *Solve your problem.*

Yes—solve your problem.

You see, Mrs. Boys knew two important secrets:

1. Kids are capable of making smart choices.
2. Kids learn more skills when they solve their own problems.

As an expert in child development, I couldn't agree more with Mrs. Boys. When children are able to make their own decisions based upon accurate information, they tend to go with better choices in the future.

So, what does *solve your problem* have to do with cell phones? Well, just about everything. Your parents will help monitor your actions on your smartphone. That is good because it takes time to learn how to be safe and kind in a digital world. Even adults have to keep learning about changes on the internet, with social media and privacy settings. However, there is no way your parents can prevent you from making some big mistakes. They will not be with you on the bus to school. They will not be with you when you are at your best friend's house. Even with controls set up for your safety, there will be millions of decisions you will have to make on your own.

In other words, you (and only you) will have to make good choices. I am certain you can make them, because you are smart and capable when given the facts. This book will help by teaching you what you need to know.

Caring for Your New Phone

Smartphones can be an expensive investment. What that means is, they cost a lot of money, so you should try to take good care of your phone. There are a few ways to make sure your phone stays safe.

MAX: "Have one place you put your phone when it is in your backpack. That way you always know where it is."

JACK: "Buy a good case. I picked out a really cool case—it was neon green with a sick alligator. But my parents made me get a boring one because they said it was 'drop proof with screen protection.' 'Whatever,' I said. Well, I drop my phone a lot. Don't tell my parents, but they were right. I need the toughest case."

BENNI: "Oh, and check all of your pockets before jumping in a pool. My cousin made this mistake. Twice."

Try to have a routine for where your phone goes at different parts of your day. Think about where to put it after school and where to charge it. If you always put it in the same place, it is more difficult to lose.

Phone Etiquette

Before we get into some of the more difficult topics, let's start with something fun—phone etiquette. Now, I know "etiquette" sounds sorta fancy and snobby, not unlike the French word for snails (that'd be *escargot*—and they're slimy and icky). But "etiquette" is just another way of saying, "Hey, use your manners." And knowing when to answer your phone or respond to a text (and when to ignore it for a little while) usually depends on etiquette.

SOFIA: "Here's an important tip: When your parents call, always answer the phone (unless you are in the bathroom. In that case, call them right back when you finish)."

It is very normal to want to look at your phone when it buzzes. But it isn't always a good idea to do so. Let's say Grandma is visiting from Florida and you and your family are at dinner. Maybe you're all eating hamburgers, and Grandma is telling a story about when her best friend in high school quit the knitting club. Then—your phone pings! I know it can be tempting, but taking time to look at your device might make Grandma feel like you don't even care that she is there. (Grandparents aren't really down with the "I'd love to listen to you, but Samantha just DMed me a photo of her new kitten and it's so cute" excuse.) It often hurts people's feelings when it seems like your phone gets all your focus. And nothing makes parents madder than when they are asking for your attention but you keep looking at your phone. Trust me on this. I'm a parent.

Also, there are some places it's just unthoughtful to take a call. Imagine you're in the movie theater, and Thor is about to soar into the air, break out his hammer, and go after Loki, and you've been waiting for this moment for the last hour, and suddenly—BLEEP! BLEEP! BLEEP! BLEEP! BLEEP!—the phone belonging to the person behind you starts to ring. And then the woman is talking! Loudly! About her hair appointment with someone named Meredith! It's the absolute worst. You *do not* want to be that lady.

So it's important to realize there is a time and place to answer a call and a time and place to put the phone down or, even better, turn it off. Be aware of your surroundings. Are you inside a restaurant with family members, or are you by yourself in your room? Before answering, take one second and ask yourself, "Is this a good time to use my phone?"

SIDE TIP

Every phone has a way to turn off the ringer (sound) and a way to stop notifications from popping up. Take a minute to learn about these functions so you can show good phone etiquette when it is needed.

BENNI: "This is my biggest problem. If I hear the little 'ding,' I have to pick up my phone and respond to it right away. I've learned to just put my phone away during meals and family time so I don't feel the urge to respond."

MAX: "Last year I had a bowling birthday party. I was so excited. All of my friends were on their phones the whole time. It was such a bummer."

As a general rule, try to connect to the people in your life when they are with you. As fun as it is to text with a group of friends or scroll through amazing dunk videos on TikTok, when you are busy doing that, you may miss what is happening in real life. So work toward focusing on the people around you rather than on your phone. Yes, I know it can be hard. Sometimes when we are bored or in awkward situations it's easier to just look at our phone. But try to live more in the moment. I promise things get a lot less uncomfortable with practice. Also, it's not very nice to be with one friend but texting another friend. It can be hurtful.

Here's a chart to help you figure out when to answer your phone and when to leave it alone. Fill this out and talk about it with your grown-up. The answer key is at the end of the chapter.

	ANSWER IT	LEAVE IT
1. Mom or Dad calls		
2. The phone rings during dinner		
3. When you are rushing to get ready for school		
4. A friend texts past your bedtime		
5. Your sister texts *HELP*		
6. An adult who watches you (like a babysitter or grandparent) calls		
7. An unknown number calls		
8. When you are doing your homework		
9. At a birthday party		
10. In school		
11. When you are home on the weekend with not much to do		

There is one more note I want to offer on phone etiquette. It is polite to answer the phone by saying, "Hello," not "Hey" or "Yo" or "What's up?" or . . . you get the idea. Of course, you can be more informal with your friends. Also, don't forget your manners when it is time to get off. Say, "I've got to go. Talk to you later," rather than just hanging up or rushing off.

Screen Time—How Much Is Too Much?

It used to be easier to limit screen time for kids mostly because there just wasn't a whole lot of opportunity. But now screens are everywhere. We use them to talk to and play with our friends. We use them for schoolwork and to watch Netflix. We use them on and off all day, every day. That's part of life. However, that doesn't mean we don't have to be mindful of our use.

TRACKING SCREEN TIME

Did you know that most phones help you monitor how much time you spend on calls, apps, and texting? It might be a good idea to check out this feature to make sure you are not using your phone more than you really want to. How much time is the right amount of time? Well, that's complicated. It really depends on when you are using your phone and what you are doing on it. I'll talk more about knowing when it's too much in Chapter 7.

Excessive cell phone use can affect your mood and sleep. It can make you feel sad and worried and make it difficult to concentrate (more on this in Chapter 7: Taking Care of You). It's a good idea to monitor how your phone makes you feel at different times of the day and when using different apps and types of media. That way you can notice your mood and make changes as needed.

Screen-Free Time

While it can be very tempting to constantly connect to your friends from school, it is also important to take a break. Being involved in the drama from school or your friend group can get exhausting.

MAYA: "There is always someone mad at someone else in my text group. Sometimes millions of texts go back and forth. It's so distracting when I'm trying to do my homework. My mom and I decided to turn my phone off for a few hours after school. It actually gives me a little break. The drama can wait."

Maya offers a great tip based on her experience. When you first get your phone, it's a good idea to think about times when you want to turn it off. Some suggestions are:

o   When you have to focus on something important

o   When a friend is visiting

○   When you are having a meal

○   When you are going to sleep

I'll talk so much more about sleep in Chapter 6. However, just a little tidbit here: Sleep experts recommend kids and adults turn off all electronics at least an hour before going to sleep. It helps the brain know it's time to shut down.

Most children, and many adults, like to charge their devices in their rooms. Kids like using their phone as an alarm clock. They often feel more comfortable having it nearby when they sleep. But for me, that's a big no-no. Like, a *really, really, really* big no-no. You will learn why also in Chapter 6. But for now, just focus on finding a place away from your room to charge at night.

Digital Contracts

Many parents like to sign a contract with their kids when they buy their first smartphone. A contract is just an agreement of rules and guidelines. Kids and parents both sign the contract so everyone is on the same page. There are so many different items that can go into a contract. I will give lots of ideas in Appendix C: Sample Contract Items. Signing a contract isn't necessary. But it can be helpful, especially in the first year after getting a phone.

(Answer Key for Answer It or Leave It: 1. Answer It, 2. Leave It,
3. Leave It, 4. Leave It, 5. Answer It, 6. Answer It, 7. Leave It,
8. Leave It, 9. Leave It, 10. Leave It, 11. Answer It)

CHAPTER TWO

WORDS MATTER

ONE OF THE MOST FUN PARTS ABOUT HAVING A SMARTPHONE IS BEING ABLE TO TEXT YOUR FRIENDS. Texting is not like regular chats you have with the people in your life. It's abbreviated (that means it's short). That's really important to remember. Texting is not a substitute for real connection or deeper conversations with your grandparents, your coach, or your teacher. It's just a fun, quick message.

Kids text:

o   To make plans with friends. *Hi, are you free this weekend?*

o   To ask a quick question. *Is the science project due tomorrow?*

o   To provide needed information, like a friend's phone number or an address for a parent to pick you up.

o   Just to chat with a friend. *How was the movie last night?*

Sounds simple, right? Well, there's a little bit more to it than typing out words and pressing send. Here's a look at a conversation between Max and Maya that didn't go as planned.

Max

Maya, can I ask you a question
about the math homework?

Maya

Max

Maya? Where r u?

Maya

Max

MAYA???? HELP???

PLEASE write me back. I need
your help.

Are you ghosting me? Are you
mad at me?

Maya

Sorry Max. I had my phone off.
We were at dinner. How can I
help you?

Max assumed that because he had his phone and
was able to text, Maya was also available. But she wasn't.
Instead of realizing Maya was busy, Max immediately
assumed Maya was mad and ignoring his texts. She
wasn't. It is a common misunderstanding.

When you are sitting around with your friends at
school or at a party, you can see their faces when they
talk. You can see if they look sad or have been crying.

You can see if someone is laughing or joking. You can see if someone is serious about something. Facial expressions, how we carry our body, and even the tone of our voice all help us understand the words we hear by putting them in context. These are called *social cues*. Just like a stop sign instructs us how to behave, the same is true of social cues.

When you are texting, you cannot see any of that. It can be very easy to misread a text or form the wrong understanding of the feelings behind the words. To avoid this, it is helpful to follow a few simple rules while texting:

- **Avoid bad news:** Since we don't know how someone will react or if they will need support, it's best to call someone to share the news.

- **DON'T USE ALL CAPS:** When people receive messages in all-capital letters, they can be read like someone is screaming.

- **Assume good intentions:** Sometimes you may read a text and feel hurt or sad. It is possible that you may have misread or missed the context. It happens to everyone. Remember, there are no facial expressions or voices to help you know the tone. When in doubt, assume a positive tone.

- **Use emojis and images to help with context:** Besides using words, it can be fun to express ourselves using pictures and symbols. In fact, adding an emoji or meme to texts helps the reader understand the emotions of the post. Plus, it can be cool to make avatars that look like you or use funny symbols to lighten up a text.

Emoji: An image that represents aspects of our body, feelings, and lives. It is used to express something more than just using our words. Here are some popular emojis. Can you guess what they express?

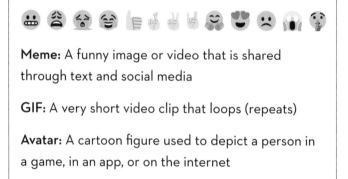

Meme: A funny image or video that is shared through text and social media

GIF: A very short video clip that loops (repeats)

Avatar: A cartoon figure used to depict a person in a game, in an app, or on the internet

Nothing Is Private

Texting often feels like a private conversation between two people. But texting is different than conversation in an important way—it's all written down.

Once you type out words and send them, you lose control of what happens with those words. That text can easily be shown to anyone. It can be copied and sent to others in seconds. Imagine if you wrote someone a private note in school, only to find out the note was shared with everyone in gym class. When we are alone typing things to friends, it's easy to open up or say something we might regret later.

To avoid having someone use your words in a way you didn't intend, try to keep your texts simple. Thinking before typing can help. Also, ask yourself this question: Would I be proud to say these words on the loudspeaker at school? If the answer is no, then maybe don't send that text.

Cyberbullying

Bullying someone through texts, social media, or the internet is called *cyberbullying*. In a way it's much easier to do online than in person. It takes only a second to send a few mean words. There is no social pressure to be nice when we are alone in our rooms. Just because it's easy to do doesn't mean it doesn't have a large impact.

There are many ways to be unkind online:

○   Spreading rumors or gossiping about someone

- Sharing without permission a picture of someone that is unflattering or mean

- Texting unkind or threatening words

- Creating fake profiles on social media with someone's name

- Telling a secret with the intention of hurting

- Posting mean comments on someone's social media posts

Here's an example that was hurtful to Max when he heard what had been said about him.

Jack texts Benni:

Jack

Hey Benni. Did you hear what happened to Max?

Benni

No!!! What happened?

Jack

He fainted right before lunch. Like he was totally out of it. I heard it was from too much vaping.

Benni

Really? No way. Gross. I didn't know he vapes.

Jack

Me either. But that's what I heard at lunch.

Benni immediately texts Maya:

Benni

Maya, did you hear what happened to Max?

Maya

I was there. I felt so badly for him. It was scary.

Benni

Is it true that he was vaping?

Maya

WHAT? No he has diabetes. His sugar went low and that makes him pass out.

Benni

Oops. I shouldn't have texted that. Sorry. I will check on Max.

Jack's text to Benni probably wasn't the best judgment. While he didn't say anything mean, he was gossiping in a way that wasn't very nice to Max. Benni added in gossip from school and then shared it with Maya. What Benni and Jack should have done was text Max to see if he was OK. I imagine that passing out in school was probably not very fun for Max. Adding lies and gossip to that situation will only make him feel worse.

MAYA: "A friend of mine had a picture of me that made me feel uncomfortable. She knew I hated it. So when she was mad at me, she would threaten to send the picture to our friends. I asked her to delete it, but she wouldn't. Eventually she did send it to our friends. Everyone told her that what she did was mean. She finally deleted it. It was really hurtful to me."

Whenever I'm texting, I try to think to myself, "Would I be embarrassed or upset if this text was shared with other people? Would someone else think this wasn't very nice?" If the answer is yes, I delete the text or make a better choice.

Sometimes cyberbullying can be a lot more serious than gossip or a few mean texts. Students have been harassed and bullied through texts for being different. Maybe it is because the student identified as gay or transgender. Or it could be for being Jewish or Muslim. Or for having a disability. Or just for being different in some way.

Cyberbullying can even be a crime. When hate speech becomes threatening or encourages someone to harm themselves, it can break the law. When that has happened, students have been expelled from school, forced to pay fines, or even sent to jail.

Decide to be an upstander. That's not only someone who wouldn't cyberbully; it's also someone who speaks out to support and protect other kids from being victims. If you have a friend who may be considering a mean text or comment, say something. You don't have to be harsh. Just tell your friend that you don't support sending that kind of message.

Privates Are Private

OK, I know you've probably been taught this already. However, it's kind of worth mentioning again, especially in relation to cell phones.

Did you know that it is against the law to share pictures in which a child (someone under the age of eighteen) is naked? It's illegal even if only a part of a child's privates is showing. And it is illegal to have those pictures on your phone even if you don't share them.

You might be thinking, "That's so crazy. Why would anyone share naked pictures?" Well, sharing naked pictures is called *sexting*. Sometimes teenagers do this in dating relationships, thinking the pictures will stay private. But as you've already learned and we will discuss more in Chapter 3, nothing you send is private. It is up to the person who receives the text to obey your wishes. Sadly, sometimes that doesn't happen.

Here is what you need to know about sexting:

o   Never send a naked or even partially naked picture of yourself to anyone.

o   If someone asks you for a naked picture, firmly say no. If that person continues to ask, block the number.

o   If someone texts you a naked picture, delete it right away and talk to your parents about it.

The person who sent that to you may need help to understand how serious it is to send naked pictures.

o   It is never OK to take a picture of someone when they're naked without their permission.

Cyberbullying: Sending, sharing, or posting anything mean, harmful, hurtful, or false about someone online, in an app, or through texting

Doxing: Giving out someone's contact information, including their physical address, phone number, or email address, without permission, for the purpose of causing harm

Sexting: Sharing pictures that show private parts or a naked person

---

It's Not All Bad News

There is one special advantage of texting that can be helpful to you: texting your parents when you need help or have a concern. Sometimes opening up about a problem can be genuinely hard. It might be something embarrassing or just so tough to say. Texting can be an easy way to start a conversation with your parents. It can break the ice, and then once that happens parents and kids can talk away from the phone.

My daughter and I have often used this technique when I can see she's struggling with something but can't yet talk about it. I'll just say, "Text it to me." She might be sitting right next to me. Still, it's easier for her to text. Once she does, the rest of the conversation flows much more comfortably.

Takeaway Tips

o   Don't text when you are angry or upset (unless it's to talk to your parents).

o   Don't spread rumors or share mean content.

o   Be an upstander.

o   Call rather than text a long story or a response to a question. That way, there's less room for mistakes or misinterpretations.

o   When in doubt, assume a positive tone. Avoid assuming the worst.

CHAPTER 3

PRIVATE EYES

THE WORD *PRIVATE* HAS MANY MEANINGS.

MAX: "I have private parts covered by underwear."

BENNI: "A secret is private. It means I don't tell anyone."

MAYA: "My dad says I am a private person. I don't like to share a lot of personal stuff with others."

SOFIA: "My neighbor has a sign that says 'Private property. Keep out.'"

JACK: "My mom says that in the military they call private information 'classified.' She is not allowed to tell me certain things, even where she is sometimes."

Private basically means *you* control how something is shared. This is one of the most important concepts to learn when starting to use your smartphone or the internet. Sharing little pieces of information about your life may seem like no big deal. Who really cares where you live or the date of your birthday? Well, *you* should care who knows that information.

Let me explain . . .

Every time you play a game, look up a video on YouTube, browse Instagram for cute puppy pictures, log in to an app, or even when you google "How to make the best chocolate chip cookies in the world," you are leaving behind information about yourself. Have you ever noticed how YouTube suggests videos that you might like—and, in fact, you *do* really like what they pick out for you? That's because YouTube has ways of monitoring your habits and discovering little tidbits about your likes and dislikes. Those tidbits are called *data*.

Every time you type a word, tap on a link, or open an app, you are sending data to different companies.

○ Google uses your data to create ads for stuff they think you might like.

○ Amazon uses your data to help you find more items to buy.

o   Apple Music uses your data to suggest songs you might enjoy.

o   Netflix uses your data to help you find movies and shows to watch.

o   Starbucks uses data to find stores located in your area so you can order on their app. They also might use your data to remind you there is a sale on your favorite drink or sandwich. (They know exactly what you like from your data.)

JACK: "The other day I googled this toothpaste my dentist recommended. The next day it showed up as an ad on Amazon. It's so crazy."

Every single thing you do on the internet leaves a record. That's called a *digital footprint*. It leaves a mark even after you turn off your phone. You can never erase that footprint. And you can never know exactly how that footprint will be used in the future. That's why it is so important to be careful about how you use your device and what you share.

Phishing, Scammers, and Hackers

Sometimes things are not as they seem. There are some people online who do not think of your best interests. They try to get to know you and find out personal information for some pretty terrible reasons.

HOT TIP: IT'S NOT PRIVATE

Assume anything you send in text or email or even in messages in an app is not private. Anything sent can be screenshot and shared with your parents, with your school principal, with the world. So, if you wouldn't want your words or pictures released to the world, think carefully about what you send.

MAX: "People try to trick you. That's called a scam. I was playing video games online with a boy I thought was my friend. He turned out to be an adult who pretended to be a kid. I realized I talked about a lot of personal stuff with this person. I told my parents, and we were able to block him. I've learned to be more careful to verify whether someone is an actual friend."

MAYA: "Some people try to steal from you. My grandpa gets a lot of calls and texts saying his credit card was stolen and they need his personal identification code to send him a new card. These people do not have my grandpa's card. They lie to try to trick him so they can steal his money."

People who use computers to obtain access to your private information are called *hackers*. *Scammers* are people who lie in order to steal something. There are many creative ways scammers try to find out your personal information. Sometimes they send texts or emails or make phone calls pretending to be a real company, like your bank or doctor's office. A false attempt to obtain your personal data is called *phishing* (pronounced like *fishing*), and they can be challenging to spot.

Scammers may say there is a balance to be paid or a problem with an account. (**BENNI**: *"Like your mom owes money or didn't pay a bill."*) Or they might tell you there is an exciting gift waiting "just for you!"—and all you have to do is just confirm one small piece of information.

MAX: "There are a lot of scams for Fortnite V-Bucks. I almost fell for one. A pop-up said, 'Click here for a code for your FREE Fortnite V-Bucks.' I remembered my dad saying, 'Nothing is free. Usually, it's a scam to get your personal information.' I really wanted those free V-Bucks, but then I realized the offer wasn't real."

Calls, emails, and texts from scammers can look very official. But there are ways to double-check before giving out any information:

o   If you DO NOT have an account with a company—say, Netflix or PlayStation—then just hang up or delete the message or email.

o   If you DO have an account with the company—like a gaming account—just take the information down and go tell your parents. They can contact the company directly. That way you can verify who you are talking to.

When in Doubt, Keep It Private

There is some information that should be kept *TOP SE-CRET* because the consequences of sharing are big:

Social Security number—That's a unique identification number every American receives when they are born. If that number is stolen, you cannot get a new number, so it is super important to safeguard it like you would

HOT TIPS

- You may have people you consider friends from playing online video games. Never give out your personal information like your phone number, address, birthday, etc.

- If a "friend" starts asking inappropriate questions or trying to get secrets out of you, they are not a friend. Block them.

- Never click on a link sent to you from a stranger until you verify the source. Opening some links can allow others to access the private information on your phone. Even if just as a joke, don't reply to people who are scammers.

- If you don't know the contact, you do not have to answer the text. It isn't rude. It's smart and safe to ignore a text from someone you do not know.

an expensive diamond ring. Show no one, not even your best friend. Tell no one unless you carefully verify why it is needed (and only do this with a grown-up).

Birthday—Your birth date is an important identification for school and medical records, bank information, credit cards, and other documents. Make sure you tell only your friends (the ones you know in real life) and family this information.

Location—Some people on the internet use your location to potentially put you in danger. Don't share your home address or school with anyone you don't know personally. This will mean not tagging pictures with your location and making sure there isn't information about you in a photo. I'll talk more on this in the next chapter.

Full name and phone number—Your phone number can be connected to your home address, so for safety it should *not* be given out to strangers. Also, giving out your number can lead to a lot of phishing messages. Your last name can also give clues to your home address.

SOFIA: "Before I share anything personal, I ask myself, 'Am I sure this is a safe person or place to post this information?' If I am ever unsure or have a funny feeling, I don't do it."

Remember, you can always ask a trusted grown-up for advice or help.

> ## HOT TIP
>
> There are times when it is necessary to give out your personal information. For example, when you want to buy something or join an app or download a game. Make sure to always ask a grown-up if it is a safe place to share that information.

MAYA: "One time I took a funny selfie in my room. I posted the picture on Instagram. When my sister saw the picture, she realized that my school ID was visible. I hadn't even realized. I quickly took the picture down."

In this picture, can you find five pieces of identifying information about Maya?

Passwords, Usernames, and Profile Pictures

On your smartphone or computer, you will have lots of personal information. That's just fine. But you should protect these devices with a password. A *password* is a group of letters and numbers that is used to restrict access to information on your devices. *Usernames* are connected with passwords to sign up for games, websites, and accounts.

Passwords and usernames help protect our identity and information from scammers and hackers. Passwords are also vital to protect us if our phones are ever lost or stolen. Many people choose passwords that are easy to remember. That is, of course, important. But it is equally important to pick something that is hard for others to guess and usernames that don't give away your personal information.

Here's a list of do's and don'ts for passwords and usernames to make sure you are extra careful:

DO	DON'T
Do choose meaningful letters and numbers that are easy for you to remember but not easy for others to guess.	Don't use your birthday, phone number, or home address.
Do have at least eight characters.	Don't make it short.
Do use at least one lowercase and one uppercase letter ("PaRkEr" instead of "Parker").	Don't use all lowercase or all CAPS.

DO	DON'T
Do use at least one special symbol: * ! # @.	Don't use only letters and numbers.
Do vary your passwords. That way if one password gets exposed on one site, it doesn't put all of your accounts at risk.	Don't use the same exact password for all accounts.
Do keep your passwords private.	Don't give your passwords to anyone, not even to your best friend.
Do use a number or symbol in place of a random letter. For example, use: 3 for E @ for a ! for I For example, "P!nk" instead of "Pink" or "Fr!3nd" instead of "Friend."	Don't repeat letters.
Do use a favorite word you will remember.	Don't use your name or the name of anyone in your immediate family.
Do wait until you are on your phone or computer at your home before signing in.	Don't sign in using your password on any public computer or on someone else's device (your information can be stolen easily on public Wi-Fi or a public computer).
Do use a password to protect your phone, or use fingerprints or facial recognition to keep it secure.	Don't leave your phone or computer without password protection.

Here are a few ideas for a password that are not your name, address, or birth date. For an even stronger password, combine two of the choices from the letters column, one from the numbers column, and use a symbol.

LETTERS	NUMBERS	SYMBOLS
Your dog's name	Favorite athlete's number	#
Your teacher's name		$
	Your mom's or dad's birthday	%
Your best friend's name		^
	Your favorite number	&
Favorite book character	Your sports jersey number	*
		+
Favorite Disney movie	The number of Super Bowls your team has won	!
		(
Favorite athlete	The number of Pokémon cards you own	)
Favorite song title		/
	The number of legs of everyone in your home, including your animals (my house has four people and one dog, so that's twelve)	{
Favorite color		}
Favorite ice cream flavor		[
		]
Favorite class in school		

If I were to make a strong password from this list, here's what I could do:

My best friend's name, then my mom's birthday, then my favorite color. If I put in some uppercase and lowercase letters and a symbol, it might look like this: ELLie1028pInK*. (Don't worry, this is not my real password or even my mom's real birthday. It's just an example.) Notice I don't put the numbers at the end.

It's common to put the numbers at the end, so people trying to guess your code will assume that. Putting numbers somewhere within the letters helps make your password much harder to deduce. Now take a moment and think about a good option for your password.

It's All About Consent

Being a good *digital citizen* (a person who uses the internet and technology) means not sharing other people's private information. Before sharing a picture or a private text that someone sent you, you must ask for permission from your friend or family member to do so. This is called *consent*.

There are two parts to consent:

o   The first part is asking someone, "Is it OK with you if I do this?" You should ask for permission before taking their picture or sharing a picture or information.

o   The second part is their response of *yes* or *no*.

If the answer is *no*, you must respect that—*no matter how funny the picture is.* Your friend gets to decide what happens to their information and what is shared. If you don't ask, you cannot assume a friend wouldn't mind.

CONVERSATION BETWEEN SOFIA AND MAYA

SOFIA: I heard a crazy story about a model who took a picture of a naked older woman in their gym locker room. She posted the picture on Snapchat saying, "If I can't unsee this then you can't either."

MAYA: Wow, that's really mean.

SOFIA: Yeah, it was. She was banned from the gym. And guess what else?

MAYA: What?

SOFIA: The woman was convicted of a crime and had to do community service because she invaded the older woman's privacy. You can't take someone's picture, especially when they are naked, without permission.

MAYA: And you definitely can't post someone's naked picture. Yikes.

Just as you wouldn't share your personal information, like your birthday or location, you should also not share that information about anyone else. Releasing someone's personal information without their consent is called *doxing*, and it can be dangerous on some occasions. So, be mindful to protect your friends as much as you would protect your own information.

TRUST THAT FUNNY FEELING . . .

Sometimes we can get a nervous feeling or butterflies in our stomach. Those feelings are our body's protective response to something that might be concerning. Trust your instincts and respect your body's message. Take a moment to pause and assess what is causing that funny feeling. With smartphones, it can happen when maybe we should not post something or when we should not give out a certain piece of personal information. If you think before you act, you can prevent a mistake.

CHAPTER 4

SOCIAL MEDIA

SOCIAL MEDIA ARE APPS AND WEBSITES THAT AL-
LOW PEOPLE TO CONNECT AND INTERACT ON-
LINE IN A SOCIAL WAY. People share pictures, ideas,
interesting articles, videos, and so much more. Here are
some examples of social media you may have heard of:

- Facebook
- Instagram
- Snapchat
- TikTok
- Twitter
- YouTube
- Discord

There is much to enjoy on social media. Each app
has a slightly different focus and format. For example,
Instagram is all about sharing pictures and videos,
whereas Twitter is more about sharing short thoughts
or comments with or without a picture. YouTube allows
users to share only videos, both short and long. TikTok
allows people to share only super-short videos.

Most social media sites recommend or require users to be at least thirteen years old. But the truth is
many kids are using either their parents' or their older
brother's or sister's account. Sometimes kids also lie
about their age. I am *not* recommending that. Waiting
to join social media until you can fully understand how
it works, the rewards and the risks, is important. But I'm
still going to cover social media in this book because at

some point soon you will have your own account, and I want you to be prepared.

Profiles are generally needed to sign up for social media. A *profile* is your account or page on the app. When you sign up, you give your page a name and a short description, so people know who you are. You can decide to post or not. If you do post, that profile becomes like your very own personal scrapbook.

An important decision you need to make when signing up for a social media account is if you want to make your account public or private. If you make it public, anyone in the world can look at your posts. I don't recommend that until you are at least twenty-one years old. One aspect of your profile that you may not be able to keep private is your profile picture, name, and description. So, choose these with safety and privacy in mind. When choosing a picture for your profile, I recommend using an avatar (that's a cartoon version of yourself) or picture of your pet or something else that cannot identify you.

HOT TIP

Always keep your social media accounts private.
You can approve anyone you want to follow you.
But you can also decline or block anyone
you don't know or don't want to follow you.

A feature of social media that is almost universal is the ability to comment on posts. Interacting with people through comments is the *social* part of social media. On most apps there is an option to like (or thumbs-up) a post. This helps the person running that account know you like that bit of content.

BENNI: "I make a lot of clothes and accessories. I post them on Instagram. I like seeing so many encouraging comments. It helps motivate me to make more items to sell."

MAYA: "I watch a lot of how-to videos on art. If the video was helpful, I always leave a comment so the creator knows I'd like more videos like that one."

HOT TIP

Never post pictures of yourself or of others that:

- Are revealing

- Are embarrassing

- Show illegal behavior like drinking, smoking, or violence

- Show where you live or go to school

What's All the Hype About?

Social media is popular for a reason. It's fun. There are so many cool things you can do on social media. For example:

Follow favorite famous people and companies: It can be fun to keep track of your favorite athletes, actors, or singers on social media. It's cool to see LeBron James's life on the road with his family, Taylor Swift's cat, and the crazy stuff GoPro posts.

Stay informed: Following your school, town, or local community organizations can help you know the date of your county fair, important information about your school dance, or about an amazing art contest you may want to join.

Join groups: Let's say you love anime or drawing or robotics or building LEGO sets. You can find a group of people who also like that same thing. I promise you there is a group for people who like exactly what you like (there's even a Facebook group for people who like carving fruits and vegetables). These groups are fun to join because you can learn about new products, learn tips to improve your abilities, share your knowledge, or offer support to someone.

Use hashtags (#): A hashtag allows social media to be searched for content related to words used after the hashtag. For example, #minigoldendoodles will help you find all content on Instagram that features little dogs of the goldendoodle breed; #knitting lets you look up accounts and posts that are all about knitting. The more specific you are, the more likely it is you will get what you are looking for. For example, using #knittinganimals might be better if you want to find animals that have been knitted.

MAX: "I am part of a kids-with-diabetes group. It's only for kids who have attended the special camp I go to. I love being in this group because I can be honest about some of my tough times with diabetes, and I can also help other kids who may be just diagnosed. It's great to keep in touch during the year when we aren't at camp."

Stay connected: With social media it is easy to stay in the day-to-day lives of friends and family who live far away.

Share memories: After you share something on social media, it may come up in a memory in future years. Years ago, I posted a funny video of my daughter with whipped cream on her face. Facebook reminds me of that memory every year on the date I posted it. I love seeing that video when it comes up.

What's the Problem?

Well, there are several potential issues with kids and social media. Here are a bunch of concerns to keep in mind when thinking about joining a social media app:

Safety

The most important concern has to do with safety. Sometimes people are not who they say they are online. We talked about scammers and people phishing for your personal information in Chapter 3.

There is another kind of troublesome person on social media. Some people call them *predators*. These are adults who are looking to engage with children in an inappropriate way. Often these adults pretend to be children in order to get to know you. They may comment and like pictures. Over time you may feel you know this person because you also like their pictures, too.

Remember, if you don't know someone *in real life* (*IRL*), be very careful about letting a profile have access to you, your information, and your pictures.

- ○ If someone you *don't* know asks to meet you, don't do it. Block the account.

- ○ If they ask for pictures of you in private messages, block them.

- ○ If they ask about dating you or inquire about your age, block them.

- ○ If they want to send you a free gift, block them.

- ○ If they give you a funny feeling (always trust your gut), block them.

- ○ And tell your parents so they can help protect you.

It's a Distraction

Social media is designed to keep you engaged. Researchers have found the perfect formula to increase the amount of time people use Facebook or YouTube. They use notifications to tell you when someone liked or commented on your posts. When you see that, of course you will want to check it out. Then once you are on the app, you scroll through pictures and videos, click on links, and read articles, and all that data leads to more suggestions of content for you to click on. Before you know it, an hour has gone by, maybe more. This doesn't just happen to kids. Social media is a distraction for all of us.

FOMO

FOMO stands for **F**ear **of** **M**issing **O**ut. It's that icky feeling that comes up when you find out your friends are doing something without you. Let's say you see a post of a birthday party that you weren't invited to. It can be painful to see friends having fun when you weren't there. Or maybe a friend has gone on an amazing vacation to the Bahamas. Her pictures may make you feel jealous that she gets to have that great trip and you had to stay home for your vacation.

SOFIA: "I get FOMO when I know another friend is sleeping over at Maya's house."

MAYA: "The funny thing is, that also happens to me when someone else is sleeping at Sofia's house."

Being on social media means seeing inside other people's lives. Sometimes that's really cool and fun. Other times it brings up feelings of sadness, depression, anxiety, or just FOMO.

There's No Break from Being Social

Being social is great. Having friends and spending time with them is part of what makes life entertaining. But believe it or not, there can be too much time together. Sometimes people need a break from one another.

JACK: "I totally get this. I am really good friends with my neighbor Tom. He comes over all the time to play basketball. Most of the time I'm cool with it. But sometimes I want to play with another friend or I just want to shoot baskets by myself. It's hard to tell him not to come over."

Jack is describing what happens when he is face-to-face with his friend. But the same thing happens online. Too much together time isn't always a good thing. Social media makes it difficult to limit socializing.

It's Not Real Life

Most people on social media present a *part* of their life but not *all* aspects of it. What we see when we scroll through pictures and videos is often carefully chosen to show the best version of a person's life. Imperfections and personal issues are often missing on social media. It makes sense. Why would anyone bother posting boring or unattractive pictures? But what happens is that we see an unrealistic view of another's life. That starts to feel not so great after a while.

When we see picture-perfect faces and houses and vacations and cars, it may make our own lives seem kind of blah. Now there are all kinds of fun filters to use to make silly pictures. But many of the filters also work to remove pimples and smooth out wrinkles. They make people look more polished. Again, that's not how we look in real life.

Some people on social media are called *influencers*. These are people who are paid to make videos or post pictures talking about a product or vacation location or food. It's a kind of advertising, but sometimes it's not as obvious as a commercial on television. Influencers might post about their favorite skin cream or about a favorite Disney ride or about their favorite beach resort. Every time someone likes or clicks on a link in their post, they get paid. They may or may not use the hashtag #ad. It's important to know who is an influencer because they may not be honest about their likes and dislikes. They may pretend to have a certain expensive lifestyle. They may not even use the cream they profess to love. It's their job to try to sway your preferences or buying habits. There isn't necessarily anything wrong with that. It's just that sometimes influencers present a life or life-style that is unrealistic. They are paid to make it look like their lives are easy, fun, beautiful, peaceful, etc. But in reality, they are putting on a limited personality for the purpose of getting you to buy into their products.

Sometimes all the picture-perfect lives we see make us feel depressed or anxious or back to FOMO. These aren't very good feelings. Whereas you may be perfectly happy with the way you look before joining Instagram, once you see all the pretty people with perfect lives, you may start to feel less good about yourself. That's a shame, because most of the people you see on Instagram often don't look like that either. They use camera angles and filters to change their look. I promise you—Olivia Rodrigo doesn't wake up with flawlessly placed curls, and Drake isn't always heading to a fancy event. Even the most gorgeous, most put together, most famous star must use the toilet, wash the dishes, and take a shower. Life isn't glamorous at all times.

There is nothing wrong with wanting to look our best or thinking carefully about which images we choose to show online. But it's important to realize that we also must be happy with our real lives. If social media starts to change that, it's time for a break. More about this in Chapter 7 on self-care.

Takeaway Tips

- Keep location access turned to Never.

- Turn off notifications on all social media apps.

- Remember that social media isn't real life.

- Be careful with whom you share information about yourself.

- Keep all accounts private.

- Message only with people you know IRL.

- Even if your account is private, it can still be screenshot and shared. Be mindful of what you share.

CHAPTER 5

TO GOOGLE OR NOT TO GOOGLE

OH GOOGLE, HOW I LOVE YOU.

I'm a curious person. So I love being able to google just about anything. Yesterday I googled a recipe for soba noodle salad. (I found one with peanut sauce in *The New York Times*. It was delicious.) I use Google Maps for directions pretty much every day. Today I used Google to find a new swimsuit.

SOFIA: "I google how to spell words or what they mean."

MAYA: "I use Google to find help with math and also to learn new art techniques."

JACK: "Today I googled the score of the Lakers game. I told my dad the Lakers would win by twenty, and they did."

Google is a *search engine* that scans the internet for information. You probably know this already, but it's an incredible resource. Every day Google handles 3,500,000,000 searches. That's 3.5 *billion*. Searching Google is part of everyday life. Chances are if you have a question, Google has the answer. You can search for websites, videos, images, and news.

It's Not All Google Goodness

As powerful as Google is, it is not entirely a safe space. The problem with such a powerful resource is that it isn't regulated. Anyone can make a website and post just about anything they want. There is likely information that you may not be ready to see.

Some examples of things you may not be prepared for:

o   Videos showing violent scenes

o   Information for illegal and dangerous activities

o   Inappropriate adult content such as pornography (pictures of naked people)

o   Unsettling news

o   Sexist, racist, or other discriminatory content, like hate speech and slurs

o   Violence or cruelty to animals

The internet can be dangerous or even just unhelpful in several ways. One way is through *pop-ups*. Pop-ups are small windows that literally pop out of a webpage. It happens without you even clicking on something. Companies use pop-ups to sell various games or products. While that's not dangerous, it is annoying. More worrisome are the pop-up scams designed to scare you or get you to click on something that may be unsafe for you or your phone or computer. The pop-up may say a virus has infected your phone or computer. Or it may say you've won something special.

Congratulations. You've won an Amazon gift card. Click here to claim your prize.

Your Apple iPhone is infected by ten viruses. Immediate action is required to prevent it from spreading and infecting sensitive data like your passwords and private information.

Just like I mentioned in Chapter 3, these are phishing attempts to gain access to your phone and personal data. Be aware, because, I promise you, these scammers are very good at their work. The pop-ups can be confusing and scary.

Always close pop-ups carefully. Use the tiny "x" that is typically in the upper left or right corner. Try to avoid clicking on a button that reads *close*. Often that does not close the pop-up. In fact, just clicking on that button may allow others access to your information. Be mindful what you click on. When in doubt, don't click. Ask an adult for help.

Another troublesome aspect of the internet is something called *clickbait*. Let's say you wanted to search Google to find a funny cat video. You might see a bunch of funny videos. But you also might see some headlines that are crazy and weird. For example:

- Cat climbs Empire State Building! You will never guess what happened next!

- Click here to find out how to get your dog to make you dinner!

- We bet you'll laugh when you see this video!

- Learn this trick and you will never need to study again!

- Get skinny without dieting!

- These are the best chicken nuggets in the world!

These are all examples of clickbait. They are headlines that are meant to tug on your curiosity and encourage you to click on them. While there may be nothing wrong with that, sometimes those videos are not what they seem. They may be fake. Worse, they may be misleading. They often incorporate bright colors and all-capital letters to catch your attention. You may think something is real when it actually isn't. Try to avoid clicking on anything that's an exaggerated claim.

JACK: "My dad always says, if it sounds too good to be true, it probably isn't true. When I see I've won something or there's a video that claims to be the best, I assume they are using those titles to get me to click. So, I just don't. It's kind of a game I play."

You Cannot Unsee Something

Because of the dangers we've just discussed, Google (like YouTube) isn't a place to just hang out thoughtlessly. It's important to think about how you use such a powerful resource.

Clickbait and pop-ups are generally annoying and potentially harmful. But the real danger of internet searches is seeing something disturbing by accident. Once you see something, it's impossible to erase the memory. You cannot unsee something. That means if you google something scary or inappropriate, you will have to deal with the consequences of seeing something that upsets you.

MAYA: "One time I clicked on a news story about World War II. I was working on an assignment for history. I opened an article that was all pictures of bodies from the Holocaust. It is an important story. But I was not at all ready to see those pictures. I had a really hard time sleeping that night."

MAX: "This is kind of embarrassing, but one time I accidently clicked on pornography. It showed adults naked doing all kinds of stuff that I didn't understand. It was waaaayyy too much for me to see. I was upset about it and not completely sure how it happened. So, I told my dad. He didn't freak out. We had a long talk. Now I know not to click on it, and if it comes up by accident, to quickly close the website."

Can It Wait?

There is a very simple process that will help you prevent an accidental click on something inappropriate. It's called "Question–Wait–Answer," or QWA for short. Sometimes it's easy in the heat of the moment to just click here and click there without putting much thought into what you're doing. But taking five seconds to pause and think about your actions will help greatly in managing your impulses.

Here's how QWA works. There are three steps:

First: Before you act (text, click, or share anything), you ask yourself a question. In the case of googling or clicking on something, you would ask, *Am I prepared for this?*

Second: Before answering, you take a five-second break to think. Just holding off for a moment can help you make better decisions.

Third: After your break—and only after your break—answer your question.

This technique is certainly good for managing Google urges. But it also works in thinking through a text to a friend. Maybe before sending that quick, angry response, use QWA to take five seconds to ask yourself if you misread the text or if you should send something that could be misread. Or maybe someone is pressuring you to send an inappropriate text yourself. QWA will be extremely helpful in giving you a few moments to consider the impact.

Search Engine: A software system that can search the World Wide Web for information. Google is just one example of a search engine. Bing and DuckDuckGo are other examples.

Clickbait: A headline designed to be catchy and encourage a click on the article or website

Pop-ups: A form of online advertising that pops up on the screen in a smaller window or box. Pop-ups can be harmless or dangerous, so they should be treated with caution.

> **Propaganda:** Misleading or biased information
> used to influence and manipulate people's beliefs,
> opinions, and actions

Not the Whole Truth

There is one more problem with the internet that we should discuss. Not everything on the internet is true. What you see can be opinion. Sometimes people exaggerate or manipulate videos, so they are not what they seem. Sometimes people even flat-out lie to purposefully spread misinformation. That's called *propaganda*, and it's used to influence and manipulate people's beliefs, opinions, and actions.

Here's a recent headline: "Microsoft co-founder Bill Gates planning to use microchips in COVID vaccine to work as tracking devices." This is untrue. Bill Gates is not interested in microchipping people. And it is currently impossible to put microchips through the needle used in vaccinations. Stories like this one are shared all over the internet on social media to discourage people from taking vaccines.

Sometimes propaganda articles have no facts or research to support the claims they make, like the popular one above about Bill Gates. It can look like clickbait. However, sometimes untrue news can be more difficult to spot because it is made to look like an actual news story. What's worse, sometimes the purpose of false news is to mislead the reader.

The good news is there are a few helpful ways to check out if information you are seeing on the internet is based on fact or fiction (untrue statements). Here are a few questions to ask yourself:

o   Who are the experts quoted in the article? Do they have professional degrees like a PhD or a medical or law degree? If yes, that is a good sign that there is some science or research behind the claims, although this is not always the case, so keep going with the following questions, too.

o   Is there another article from a reputable source (see the box on page 73) you can double-check this information with? This is helpful because one article may sound convincing, but chances are if there aren't a lot of other credible people citing the same research and conclusions, it's probably not a trustworthy article.

o   Is the article trying to sell something? News articles shouldn't be trying to get you to buy a product. Ever.

When in doubt, fact-check information. Google a person mentioned in the story and find out more. Google the source or website. If it is a well-known, reputable newspaper (*The New York Times*, *The Washington Post*, *The Wall Street Journal*) or an accredited professional association (like the Centers for Disease Control and Prevention, the American Academy of Pediatrics, the Mayo Clinic), you can probably trust the information. But don't be afraid to double-check any source of information.

HOW TO TELL IF A NEWSPAPER OR WEB SOURCE IS REPUTABLE

- Authors are identified with bylines (a line at the beginning of a news story, magazine article, or book giving the writer's name)

- Corrections of mistakes are made publicly

- Avoids clickbait headlines

- Reports facts that are not highly debatable

- Articles disclose sources who are experts or who are sharing firsthand knowledge

Takeaway Tips

o   Not everything you read on the internet is true. Be a careful consumer of information.

o   Pause before clicking on anything that gives you a funny feeling of worry or concern.

o   Use Question–Wait–Answer to make sure you are ready for what you are about to google.

CHAPTER 6

DREAMS, NOT SCREENS

KIDS ARE FAMOUS FOR TRYING TO DELAY BED-TIME.

SOFIA: "I'm a master at this. Just when I'm supposed to get in bed, I say I have to put something in my school bag. I need a drink of water. Or I go to the bathroom again. Or I have to tell my parents something urgent. I'm so good at it now, it makes my parents laugh."

Being told to go to sleep can feel like a punishment. Life is so fun. So much to do. So little time. Who wants to sleep when they can play? Well, I do. As much as I love life, I *love* to sleep. There is something nice about powering my brain down, having some quiet time, and resetting for the next day.

My Poppi (grandpa) used to say he was recharging his batteries when he slept. That feels like such a perfect analogy. Sleep is absolutely required for health and well-being. And not getting enough of it can cause serious problems.

The Seriousness of Sleep

We can all manage our lives just fine after one sleepless night. But if we don't get enough sleep for more than a few days, sleep deprivation sets in. That's not a good thing.

Six- to twelve-year-olds need ten to eleven hours of sleep every night. Older kids (ages thirteen to twenty-one) need nine hours per night. Take a second to calcu-

AGE	HOURS OF SLEEP NEEDED EACH NIGHT
6 to 12 years old	10 to 11 hours
13 to 21 years old	9 hours

late how much sleep you get on average every night. Are you in this range? Chances are, you are not. Maybe you are going to bed too late or waking up too early. Maybe you are waking often in the night or using electronics before or during bedtime.

Lots of research has been conducted about sleep and cell phones. Depending on the study, somewhere between 68 percent to 80 percent of teens sleep with their phones in their bedrooms. Nearly 30 percent of kids keep their phones by their pillows. Can you guess what happens at night when people (kids and adults) keep their phones so close by?

Studies show sleep is more interrupted and people sleep an hour less every night when phones are in or by the bed. You know those notifications we talked about in Chapter 4? Well, imagine being woken up from sleep every time a friend texts you or likes your post on Instagram. As soon as you see those notifications, your brain does a mental backflip. It's super exciting—but that excitement is not beneficial for sleeping.

When you don't get enough sleep or are constantly woken up throughout the night, there is an incredibly long list of side effects. Kids who don't sleep well are cranky and have a harder time dealing with emotions. That means that stuff you can normally handle with no problem might now be an issue.

JACK: "This perfectly describes me. When I don't get enough sleep my mom calls me a bear. I'm frustrated by everyone and everything. And the worst part is that I play basketball terribly. My coach can even tell when I don't sleep well."

There are lots of other issues from not sleeping well. Here are just a few:

- o Lower grades and academic performance due
   partially to difficulty concentrating and reasoning

- o More likely to gain weight

- o More depression and anxiety

- o More disorganization and problems with memory

- o Less happiness

Sleep Remission

Texting throughout the night might not seem like that
big of a deal. It isn't just the anxiety, depression, and
lowered grades due to lack of sleep that are issues. It's
also the lack of a break from the social world.

Kids who use their smartphones (or tablets and computers) in the night are sometimes called *vampers*. Research shows that kids who are vampers are also more
likely to sext (send or receive naked pictures) before
reaching their eighteenth birthday. I believe this happens
more often because our inhibitions are lowered at night.
Parents are asleep. No one is really watching. Our friends
are in their bedrooms alone. Sometimes teens make riskier
choices without social pressure or parental oversight.

Besides getting rest, sleep has one more important
function. It provides a break from life. Even kids can feel
pressure from school, friends, and family. Life can be
hard sometimes. A good night's sleep without interrup-

tions offers a mental respite from life. It's nice to also have a little time to wake up in the morning before getting hit with texts about the news of the day.

Sleep Solutions

Sleep is more than just time in bed with your eyes closed. It's time to heal and refresh. Charge your batteries, like my Poppi said. So here are some helpful ways to ensure you do get the most out of your recharge.

Charge phones, computers, and tablets out of the bedroom. Pick a place in the house and make that your charging station. Find a place with plenty of room and outlets. It feels good to have a place to put all your things, especially your electronics.

MAYA: "I actually feel so much better leaving my phone out of my bedroom at night. My friends all know I don't want to text right before bed or in the evening. It makes me feel less anxious when I go to sleep. At first it was hard to leave it in the kitchen. But now it's a relief."

It's not enough to put your devices away just before you go to sleep. **It's helpful to turn off all electronics one hour before bedtime.** Your computer and cell phone produce a blue light that interrupts your body's ability to produce a hormone called melatonin. And that's a problem because it's the melatonin that helps you feel sleepy.

This might seem obvious, but **buy an alarm clock**. There are so many fun options online. I can't tell you how many kids tell me they sleep with their phones because it serves as their alarm clock. I believe them. But that's silly. There are inexpensive options so that you can avoid the temptation to text when you should be sleeping.

The last piece of getting enough sleep has nothing to do with your cell phone. People who tend to go to sleep around the same time every night sleep better. It can be helpful to have a bedtime routine that includes turning off devices and engaging in a quiet activity like reading, playing a game, or listening to soothing music. Then brush your teeth and get in bed. Some people like to shower at night as part of their wind-down routine.

MAX: "I turn on sports talk radio on my alarm clock. I set a timer to help me fall asleep."

MAYA: "I like to read in bed with a flashlight to get ready to sleep."

Takeaway Tips

- No electronics in the bedroom within one hour of bedtime.

- Establish a healthy sleep routine, including a consistent bedtime.

- Buy an alarm clock so you don't need to use your phone to be sure you wake up on time.

- Shut off electronics one hour before bed.

CHAPTER 7

TAKING CARE OF YOU

SOMETIMES IT FEELS LIKE WE'RE SO USED TO
OUR PHONES THAT WE FAIL TO REMEMBER HOW
INSANELY INCREDIBLE THEY ARE. I mean, think
about it: With one tiny device, you can find directions
from Tulsa to Toledo, look up a recipe for homemade
waffles, watch the Knicks play the Pelicans, Zoom with
your grandma in India, edit your photos so you and Lil
Nas X are sitting together on a park bench, and chat—
face-to-face—with seventeen friends at once. The pos-
sibilities are endless.

Throughout this book I've mentioned a lot of ways
to protect yourself from the dangers of the internet,
social media, sexting, and cyberbullying. There is one
more protection I want to introduce you to—self-care.

Self-care is exactly what it sounds like. It's taking
time to care for yourself to ensure your well-being. As
I said earlier, life can be hard. School can be stressful.
Friendships can be strained. Maybe you are fighting
with your parents or siblings. Maybe you didn't do so
well on a recent exam or in an important hockey game.
When times get difficult, it is self-care activities that will
keep your physical, emotional, and mental health in
good shape.

Right about now you might be asking yourself,
"What does self-care have to do with smartphones?"
Well, a lot, actually.

In Chapter 6 I discussed some of the downfalls of sleeping with your phone. Basically, sleeping with your phone will likely result in significantly less sleep, which in turn increases the risk of depression, anxiety, and a host of other issues. For that problem, there is an easy fix. Turn your phone off an hour before bedtime and keep it out of your bedroom at night. Simple enough.

Unfortunately, sleeping with a phone isn't the only time smartphones negatively affect our mental and physical health. Let's discuss a few more areas of concern and how to combat them.

Too Much Screen Time?

I'm not really a stickler about screen time in general. The way we work, go to school, and even socialize has changed dramatically through the years. So much of what we do is online and in front of a screen. Grouping all screens together as one evil blob can be misleading. It's more helpful to take a deeper look to see what you are doing during those screen hours.

You may spend two hours online researching the rain forest for a science paper or two hours playing Candy Crush. One activity is educational. The other is just for fun. However, all screen activity when compounded together has the potential for negative effects. Research shows that more hours spent online (television, video games, and especially social media) correlates to:

o   Increases in cyberbullying and online harassment

o   Higher rates of depression (intense feelings of sadness and hopelessness)

o   Lower self-esteem (more on that in a bit)

o   Less sleep

o   Worse body image

o   Less happiness

So even though some examples of screen time may be more productive than others, it is important to keep an eye on overall time spent in front of a screen.

Opportunity Cost and Time Management

When I was in college, I learned about a concept called *opportunity cost*. An opportunity cost is what happens when you choose one activity over another.

You play Ping-Pong instead of watching TV. Or you go to a Dodgers game instead of having lunch with your brother. The cost is what you miss out on when you make a specific choice. For example, when you decide to play video games online, the cost may be less time for homework, fewer hours reading, fewer hours hanging out with friends, and less time exercising. And these costs might contribute to other costs, such as obesity, lower grades in school, and disappointing performances in sports.

The amount of time you spend offline matters—in a big way. Whether it's hanging with your friends, competing in a robotics tournament, playing on a high school lacrosse team, or learning the tuba—time offline increases happiness. And it also lowers the risk of all sorts of other problems. The goal shouldn't be to eliminate screen time from your life. That would be impossible. But it is a good idea to be mindful of the way you use your time.

The following pages show two charts. For a week, keep a log of how you spend your time when you aren't at school or doing homework. Don't judge yourself. The idea is to get an honest assessment of how you use your hours. You don't have to share it with anyone. Just live your normal life but keep track. At the end of the week, add up your totals for each activity.

Hours Spent on Leisure Screen Activities

Searching/ scrolling through videos, pictures, or social media (but not engaging) _____hours	Creating media (editing pictures, making videos, making music to share) _____hours	Watching movies or shows on Netflix, Hulu, Apple TV+, etc. _____hours
Watching YouTube _____hours	Using social media (commenting, liking, engaging) _____hours	Texting friends _____hours
Playing video games online with friends _____hours	Playing video games alone _____hours	TOTAL screen hours _____hours (add up hours from all 8 boxes)

BENNI: "I get totally sucked in when I'm on YouTube. So, I set a timer for thirty minutes. It's a nice break from homework. When the timer goes off, I know it's time to get back to work."

MAYA: "I actually deleted a few apps from my phone because I was spending too much time on games. Now if I want to play a certain one, I can access it on the computer. That is harder to do, so I end up playing much less."

Hours Spent on Leisure Activities
Not on a Screen

Playing sports _____hours	Playing with friends outside _____hours	Making art, playing music, or enjoying other creative outlets not on a screen _____hours
Clubs: Girl or Boy Scouts, robotics, LEGO League, etc. _____hours	Playground or skate park or bike riding _____hours	Other activities not on a screen _____hours
Playing with friends inside _____hours	Playing games that don't have a screen (cards, Monopoly, Risk, Life, etc.) _____hours	TOTAL non-screen hours _____hours (add up hours from all 8 boxes)

When the week of tracking is over, think about the choices you made. I'll bet there were a few areas that surprised you. Look at your two charts, and now think consciously about what changes you might like to make for the next week. If you want to lower your time on any one activity, try setting a timer when you begin. Or designate certain free times to do online activity. You can create a schedule with blocks of time for homework, outdoor or club activities, meals, and fun time.

Some phones can also help with tracking. My iPhone does daily and weekly screen-time calculations for me. It also lets me know how I'm spending my time. The following is an example of one recent week. My daily screen-time average on my iPhone was three hours and thirty-three minutes. Yikes! That is definitely more than I'd like. I also noticed that I put in the most time on Instagram, then Facebook. In one week I spent almost eight hours on just those two apps. This information was helpful—and eye-opening. Now that I know, I am much more conscious of when I pick up my phone, and I deleted Facebook from my phone. Also, the iPhone allows me to set time limits on certain apps and schedule downtime. During downtime, I can use only certain apps, which I decide on ahead of time. So I decided to allow Google Maps, texting, and phone calls during downtime.

Self-Esteem and Your Phone

The confidence you have in your abilities and worth is your *self-esteem*. When you have a high self-esteem, you feel comfortable trying new things and pushing out of your comfort zone. It helps you conquer challenges as they come up. When your self-esteem is low, you may judge yourself harshly or feel unhappy with your looks and abilities. Low self-esteem is often connected to negative body image, depression, and lower grades. That's because low self-esteem affects how we see our worth. If you don't believe you are worthy of good grades, having friends, doing well in sports, or going to college, you might make choices that aren't beneficial to you in the long run.

Unfortunately, social media can greatly impact our self-esteem. Social media presents idealistic examples of life. Remember, it only looks like picture-perfect people in perfect lives. It's not real, but we can't help comparing ourselves to that idealized image. That can hurt

our self-esteem. It can be a bummer to see all the amazing clothes, makeup, vacations, cars, homes, and lives of people on Instagram and TikTok.

MAYA: "I love scrolling through Instagram and TikTok. But I was noticing that it was stressing me out. I didn't like my hair as much. I didn't like my clothes. I was losing myself a little. I decided to take a step back and limit my time and also unfollow some accounts that were making me unhappy."

Another way social media can lower self-esteem is with likes and shares. Kids sometimes equate likes on a picture on social media with likes of oneself. They use likes to measure popularity, character, and value. That's an enormous mistake. You are way more than the number of likes and shares you may receive on a post. When you post something, it may feel gratifying to have others like it. But sometimes you can feel incredibly bad if a post is ignored or, even worse, criticized.

Just like you are so much more than the pictures you post, your self-worth should not come from likes, shares, and comments. Try to pay attention to how your mood changes when you use your phone, especially when on social media.

BENNI: "Sometimes I can get caught up in arguing with total strangers on TikTok or Instagram. The arguments are usually stupid, but they suck me in. Then before I know it

I'm yelling at my phone and getting so frustrated. My mom said I need to stop commenting on posts when they are not by my friends. I think she is right."

Focus your attention on building up your skills, getting good grades, making real relationships in real life. In the end, it's what you do offline that will make you feel good about yourself.

Your Self-Care Plan

Some people think self-care is just about getting a manicure or having a chocolate milk shake. While those activities sound like fun, they're not necessarily self-care. Self-care activities are different for everyone, but they have some similar characteristics. They are designed to take you to a calm state, help you recharge, and give you a break from the stress of life.

For self-care to be helpful, it needs to be purposeful. You need to schedule it. Find the time, because if you do not, you risk mental and physical health issues. Here are some options for what self-care is and what it is not:

SELF-CARE IS	SELF-CARE IS NOT
Exercise (walking, jogging, biking, yoga)	Mindless eating of high-calorie snacks
Meditation or mindfulness (there are some great apps, like Headspace, that can help)	Zoning out with your smartphone in your room
Spending quiet time alone	Playing video games with friends
Spending time connecting face-to-face with a friend	Going to a party
Creative hobbies (art, writing, making music, photography)	Competitive sports

SELF-CARE IS	SELF-CARE IS NOT
Asking for help	Refusing to ask for help
Getting enough sleep and having an early bedtime	Staying up late all week and sleeping in late on Sunday
Taking a bubble bath	Shopping
Finding time to do the things you love	Overscheduling
Getting outside for fresh air	Staying in your room all weekend
Hobbies that do not involve electronics	Editing photos and videos on your computer
Spreading kindness	Thinking only of yourself
Talking to an adult or friend about a problem	Keeping all feelings, emotions, and problems in

There are many more options for self-care. The important thing is to recognize that you need it. We all need to be mindful of protecting our well-being. So how can you tell it's time for some self-care? Well, when you feel stressed, grumpy, cranky, short-tempered, tired, sad, or unhappy, those are your clues that self-care is needed.

Takeaway Tips

○ Our activities on screens affect our moods and mental and physical health.

○ Self-care is vital to managing all the emotions and stresses in life.

○ Planning activities away from screens is the key to happiness and a lower risk for negative outcomes.

CHAPTER 8

THE MISTAKES YOU MAKE

HERE IS SOMETHING I KNOW FOR SURE: YOU ARE GOING TO MAKE SOME BIG MISTAKES WITH YOUR SMARTPHONE. How can I be so sure? Because every single person who has ever had a smartphone has made some giant mistakes.

Here are the most common:

o   Clicking on a link that is a scam

o   Sending a not-very-nice text in the heat of the moment then regretting it later

o   Googling something you don't know anything about and being horrified when you find out what it is

o   Accidentally giving your password, address, or personal information to the wrong person

o   Losing or breaking your phone

o   Overusing your phone

Mistakes have a bad reputation. We are programmed to try to avoid making them at all costs. But mistakes shouldn't be feared. In fact, mistakes are how we learn the most. Yes, there are consequences for mistakes. And sometimes those consequences can be upsetting and painful. That pain is actually a good thing, because a painful consequence helps remind us never to make that same mistake again.

BENNI: "I snuck my phone into my room one night when I couldn't sleep. When my mom and dad found out, they took the phone away for a week. I hated that so much. I won't do that again."

JACK: "I was forgetting my basketball uniform every week. It was making my coach crazy. He told me next time I forgot it, I would have to sit out of the game. Well, I did forget my uniform again, and I did sit out of a game. I was so mad. But it did teach me an important lesson. Now when my uniform is washed, I immediately put it in my backpack. I'm not taking any chances."

Don't be afraid of mistakes. They happen, and it is not the end of the world when they do. Just think of them as learning opportunities. No big deal.

The Learning Curve

I'm sure you've heard the saying *Practice makes perfect*. And yes, it's sort of an annoying thing to hear. But it's also true. How can you really become good at something that you have no opportunity to practice? Answer: You cannot. Practicing (and making mistakes along the way) is what builds the knowledge to do better in the future.

It is a guarantee that you will make some unwise choices with your smartphone. But each misstep will bring you closer to a place of competence (that's when you've mastered something). Just because mistakes are expected doesn't mean you can't work to minimize the damage.

A *learning curve* is the process it takes to learn something new. When you first try a new skill, the learning curve is steep. That means there's a lot to learn. When taking on a big new skill, it helps to break down the learning into more manageable steps. Don't try to learn everything and do everything all at once. That's when it becomes easier to make bigger mistakes. Instead, focus on a few areas. When you master those areas, enter into a new one.

MAYA: "When I got my phone, I decided just to add a few games and some music. I didn't want to start with social media until I was comfortable."

BENNI: "I did something similar. But in my case, I just started with Instagram for social media. I wanted to get used to one platform before trying out another. I'm so glad I did, because there was a lot to learn about staying safe, how to avoid conflict with strangers, and privacy."

Build a Safety Net

Have you ever seen scaffolding on the side of a building or the net under a flying trapeze at the circus? Those safety measures allow workers to practice and practice and practice until they don't even need a net.

A safety net is useful with technology because it helps support you as a learner. There are many ways to build a framework to ease you in. Some suggestions include:

- Using safety controls and protections set up by your parents

- Trying to learn simple apps before moving on to more complex ones

- Start by texting just one friend at a time before moving on to group chats

- Ask an adult questions before moving forward with something you don't understand

o   Set timers or use apps to minimize screen time

o   Allow parents to periodically check your phone to look for learning opportunities

The goal of scaffolding is to make the adjustments and then take the structure down. It isn't permanent. The more you learn, the less controls you need. Using support and taking your time to learn does not mean you aren't smart and capable. Knowing what you don't know and asking for help is smart. That's how you learn.

When Mistakes Happen

Learning about technology is a lifelong process. You will never be done learning, even when you are grown up. That's because technology changes so quickly. There is always a new app or scam or service update that you will have to learn. And if you are always learning, you will likely make a few mistakes along the way.

When a mistake happens, it's important to be able to talk about it with someone. That someone could be an older brother or sister, parent, grandparent, teacher, counselor, coach, or anyone you trust. You might be tempted to cover up mistakes or pretend they didn't happen. You may feel embarrassed or afraid of getting into trouble. That is understandable. No one likes to admit when they are wrong. It is true your parents might punish you or give you a lecture (but I'll try to help them not do that in my notes to them). Still, do the right thing and tell them. Smartphones are too complex with too many potential dangers for you to keep missteps to yourself.

So be brave. Speak up when you don't know how to do something. Express your concerns. Ask for help. You are living in the most exciting time to be alive, with the greatest technology the world has ever seen. It's both a golden opportunity and a big burden. However, I truly believe you can—and will—handle it well.

Be smart.

Be careful.

Be compassionate.

And, most important, be responsible.

NOTES FOR PARENTS

(KIDS, NOW IT'S TIME TO PASS THIS BOOK TO YOUR GROWN-UPS!)

Thank you for buying this book. Equipping youth with the information needed to make good choices is so important. You cannot be with your children all the time to protect them. They will have to protect themselves to some degree. However, I did want to include a few notes to help you support your children.

This Is Just a Beginning

This book is meant to be a guide to open up discussions. To keep the book manageable and interesting, it purposely presents information at an introductory level. Yet learning to be a good digital citizen isn't a one-and-done kind of situation. It's a lifelong process. Your children will not read this book and suddenly be completely safe and protected from the dangers on the internet. It is a big first step. It's just not the last step.

Learning about a new digital device takes time. The key to learning is practice. If you only give kids a totally locked-down phone, they have no opportunity to learn. But you also don't want to give them an all-access pass. A good place to start is with a few apps, games, and potentially one type of social media. You should limit screen time, their ability to download games, access to the internet, and purchasing ability, and use other precautions as well. Work together to make sure your child stays kind and safe using their new smartphone. Gradually loosen the controls to allow your children more freedom as they become more proficient and responsible.

Ongoing Digital Education

Digital current events are great dinner conversation starters. Every day there is a story about consent, data breaches, doxing, cyberbullying, privacy, and sexting. Your child may not face every situation naturally. The more real-life examples you can provide, the easier it is to learn. Newsworthy examples also show kids that these are important issues of concern even for adults. These conversations are perfect moments to gain a deeper understanding about what is going on for your child.

When talking about a news story, make sure to ask questions and listen as much as you talk. Ask if your child knows of anything like this happening in school or to a friend. Try to create an environment where you and your child are on the same team. Also, allow your child to ask any question, even if it seems basic or silly.

These talks shouldn't be lectures. This is a chance to learn what's really going on in your child's digital world. Don't miss this opportunity.

Another way to help kids gain skills is to role-play. At first, your child will not know how to write an email to a teacher or how to text a friend to make plans. They may not know how to respond to a mean text or how to comment on social media. Practicing a scenario will help your child gain skills and confidence to manage these tasks without you in the future.

Rebrand Mistakes

Your child is going to make mistakes. Some of those mistakes might have big consequences. Try not to panic. It's unlikely that any mistake at this point is going to ruin your child or their chances for a successful, happy life. Think of each mistake, even the big ones, as stepping-stones to becoming a capable adult.

Create a safe space at home to discuss digital education. That means keeping your cool when you inevitably learn about a misstep. If you get angry or accidentally shame your child for a wrong move, you will shut down future conversations. Instead of coming to you for help and advice, your child will go to friends, siblings, or, worst of all, they will have no one to turn to.

If a child seems to need more limitations on digital use, try not to make that punitive. Instead, offer these limitations as tools. For example, if your child has been struggling to get homework done, offer limited screen time hours.

Contracts

It may be tempting to come down firmly on the side of rules and regulations for the new device. Structure, rules, and consequences are all important. However, try to step back and allow your child to work through the pros and cons of various policies. Self-determination and choice foster internal motivation to abide by the rules. This is great news for parents because it means you might not have to nag or argue about obeying the rules. Your child will have buy-in. Furthermore, kids will exhibit more self-control and competence with regard to the digital world if they are part of the process of determining the rules. Wait until your child has finished this book to work on a digital contract together. You can find sample items for contracts to discuss with your child in Appendix C.

Be a Role Model

The whole *Do as I say not as I do* routine won't work with digital devices. Your children are watching you. They are seeing what you post online, including images of them. They are seeing you engrossed in a text exchange when they are trying to tell you something. They see you sleeping with your phone. Children copy what they see. So if you want your children to have good habits with their phones, then you need to show them you have good habits, too. Follow the same rules of when to answer your phone and when to ignore it as your children. And please, for your own sake, don't sleep with your phone.

Takeaway Tips

- Children will need ongoing digital education.

- Create a safe space to discuss digital issues and concern.

- Don't freak out. Keep calm and handle whatever comes up with patience and understanding.

- Model the behavior you want to see in your children.

ACKNOWLEDGMENTS

This book was imagined and written during a global pandemic. One would think it would be easy to stay home and write when there is literally nowhere else to go. But in truth, it's not as simple as it seems. There were a lot of people who encouraged me and kept me going.

My agent, Coleen O'Shea, always makes me feel like I am a priority. I am grateful for her support and consistent willingness to hop on a call whenever needed. Thank you to my editor, Sara Carder, and everyone at TarcherPerigee. I feel truly blessed to be able to publish a second book together. A gigantic thank-you to Dave Coverly for making my illustration dreams come true.

Thank you to the many parents who have offered their perspective on smartphones, children, and this book: Kopal Goonetileke, Jeanne Beaupre, Jill Kuppinger, Noel Besuzzi, Michelle Nicoloff, Michelle Woo, Kristin Shaw, Satara Charlson, Mike and Margaret Moodian, Nakisha Castillo, and Sasha Crowley.

I could not have written any of this book without my littlest advisors. These kids offered feedback and gave me the inside scoop. Thank you, Emma F., William M., and Kyelle, Kanya, and Hariel G. A special thank-you to my youngest editor, Torin Shaw, who carefully read the manuscript and gave me expert advice.

I would not have survived quarantine without the near-daily texting and support from Alison Cimmet. Thank you for believing in me and this project. Ellie Wertheim read this proposal and manuscript, offered thoughtful edits, and most of all made me feel like this was a good idea. El, you are my ride-or-die. Thank you!

Thank you to my sisters, Leah Guggenheimer and Jessica Berman, for always cheering me on or offering a pat on the back. We all need that. Thank you to my nephews, Jordan and Isaiah Williams, who are always an inspiration, and to Amelia Mae Berman for offering the most joy during a miserable pandemic. Thank you to my parents, Laura Cole and Richard Guggenheimer, for never doubting me when I say I'm going to try something new. At 101 years old my grandma Norma Shapiro learned to use an iPad. She's proof that we are never too old for a digital education.

My children, Casey and Emmett, have taught me so much of what is in this book, either through parenting them with their digital devices or from their telling me what's really going on for kids. Thank you for making it so easy to tell you to put your phones away. I'm proud of you both, always.

Jeff Pearlman, thank you for everything you took care of so I could write, for every editorial note you've given me in the past ten years, and for the foot rubs. You know what I need when I need it, even when I don't. I still couldn't ask for more. XO

GLOSSARY OF TERMS AND ACRONYMS

Avatar: A cartoon figure used to depict a person in a game or app or on the internet

Block: Remove an account from having the ability to follow, contact, or comment to your social media account

Catfish: A person who pretends to be someone else on social media

Clickbait: Content often using interesting formatting or catchy phrases to attract attention to encourage a click on a link

Cyberbullying: Mean behavior that is conducted through the internet, social media, and cell phones

Digital citizen: A person who uses the internet and technology

Digital footprint: The data and information left on the internet as a result of online activity

Doxing: Disclosing someone else's identifying or private information (like a phone number and address) on the internet, typically with cruel intentions

Etiquette: Polite behavior that is expected in relationships and society

Fact: A piece of information that is proven or known to be true

Fiction: A statement that is false

Ghosting: A sudden ending of a friendship without warning or explanation

GIF: A very short video that loops (repeats)

Group chats: Texting with more than one person at a time in the same text

Influencer: A person who is paid to influence viewers of their content, typically with regard to buying or using a product

Learning curve: The process it takes to learn something new

Opinion: A personally held viewpoint or judgment

Opportunity cost: What you miss out on when you make a specific choice to do one thing over another

Pop-ups: Small windows that pop up on the screen when using the internet

Pornography: Pictures or videos of naked people

Predators: A person who exploits (uses) another person in an abusive or dangerous manner

Profile: An account you set up on social media that contains information you choose to share

Propaganda: Misleading or biased information used to influence and manipulate people's beliefs, opinions, and actions

Push notifications: Pop-up messages that alert a user to activity on an app or social media

Screen shot: A copy of what is visible on a smartphone or computer screen

Search engine: A software system that can search the World Wide Web for information. Google is just one example of a search engine.

Search results: The list of information given by a search engine as a result of a query

Self-care: Activities that promote mental, emotional, and physical health

Self-esteem: The confidence you have in your abilities and worth

Sexting: Sharing pictures that show private parts or a naked person

Social cues: Facial expressions, how we carry our body, and even the tone of our voice, which help us understand the words we hear by putting them in context

Social media: Apps and websites that allow people to connect, in a social way

Source: Someone who provides information

Vamper: Person who uses their cell phone throughout the night

Vaping: Using an electronic device to inhale vaporized liquid

COMMON ACRONYMS (abbreviations)

Abt: About

Bc: Because

BFF: Best friend forever

BRB: Be right back

DM: Direct message (sending a text through an app like Facebook or Snapchat)

FOMO: Fear of Missing Out

FR: For real

FT: FaceTime

GTG: Got to go

IDK: I don't know

IK: I know

ILY: I love you

IM: Instant message

IMO: In my opinion

IMHO: In my humble opinion

IRL: In real life

J: Just

JK: Just kidding

L8R: Later

LOL: Laugh out loud

NBD: No big deal

NP: No problem

NVM: Never mind

Ofc: Of course

OMG: Oh my gosh

PPL: People

Prob: Probably

RN: Right now

SMH: Shaking my head

TBH: To be honest

TBT: Throwback Thursday

THO: Though

TMI: Too much information

TMRW: Tomorrow

TTYL: Talk to you later

TTYT: Talk to you tomorrow

TY: Thank you

TYSM: Thank you so much

W: With

WAY: Where are you?

WBU: What about you?

Y: Why?

YK: You know

RECOMMENDED RESOURCES FOR CHILDREN AND PARENTS

Be Internet Awesome: https://beinternetawesome
.withgoogle.com/en_us

Common Sense Media Parents' Ultimate Guides:
https://www.commonsensemedia.org/parents-ultimate
-guides

Discord Safety Center: https://discord.com/safety

Facebook Parents Portal: https://www.facebook.com/
safety/parents

Google Safety Center: https://safety.google/families

Instagram Tips for Parents: https://help.instagram
.com/154475974694511

Smart Social Resources: https://smartsocial.com/blog

Snapchat Support Staying Safe on Snapchat: https:// support.snapchat.com/en-US/article/safety-tips-resources

Snopes.com: https://www.snopes.com

TikTok Guardian's Guide: https://www.tiktok.com/ safety/en/guardians-guide

Twitter Safety and Security: https://help.twitter.com/ en/safety-and-security

YouTube Community Guidelines: https://www .youtube.com/howyoutubeworks/policies/community -guidelines/#staying-safe

SAMPLE CONTRACT ITEMS

There are many possible ideas for a cell phone contract. Here is a list of some potential items for your contract. For a downloadable sample contract and family rules, visit my website (www.thefamilycoach.com).

Child Understands and Agrees To

Etiquette

- I will not use my phone in ways that will annoy other people, such as in a restaurant, in a movie theater, at a doctor's office, or when it is otherwise inappropriate.

- I will not share anything that would make another person uncomfortable or upset.

- I will always answer texts and calls from important family members and babysitters as long as it is safe to do so.

o   I will not use my phone without permission during school hours or in the evening.

o   I will spread only friendship through texts and social media. Mean comments and texts are not allowed.

Health and Safety

o   Having a smartphone is a privilege that can be taken away for safety or other reasons.

o   I will not purchase or download anything without prior permission.

o   I will make time for activities away from my digital device.

o   I will plug my phone in a room besides my bedroom at least an hour before bedtime.

o   I will tell an adult if I am approached by a stranger on my digital device or if anything happens that makes me uncomfortable.

o   I will not share or post pictures of any private parts or naked people. If I am approached to send a picture, I will firmly say, "No!"

o   I will take care not to google something that may not be age appropriate for me.

- o   I will not communicate with anyone online or in texting that I do not know in real life.

Privacy

- o   I will not share my passwords with anyone besides my parents.

- o   I will always share my passwords with my parents until I can pay for my own cell phone plan.

- o   I understand that anything I text and share may not remain private. It can be copied and shared with the world.

Mistakes

- o   I will be honest if I am asked a direct question about my smartphone.

- o   I understand that mistakes I make on my smartphone may be embarrassing and have consequences. I will try hard to minimize mistakes by asking for help when I need it.

- o   If I lose or break my phone, I may be responsible for paying for a replacement.

- o   I understand that I may lose access to my phone temporarily as a consequence. I will not use other devices to text or use social media while

I am on a break imposed by my parents or guardian.

Parent/Guardian Understands and Agrees To

- o   I understand that learning digital safety is a process and takes practice.

- o   I will be nonjudgmental and will keep calm when mistakes are made.

- o   I will discuss rule changes with you to make a plan that takes your point of view into consideration.

- o   I will check your phone periodically and provide ongoing education to support learning.

- o   I will be a good role model by putting my phone down during family time, not sleeping with my phone, and not texting while driving.

Signed by:

_____ Name and Date

_____ Name and Date

_____ Name and Date

ABOUT THE AUTHOR

Dr. Catherine Pearlman is the founder of The Family Coach® and a licensed clinical social worker who has been working with children and families for more than twenty-five years. She holds a PhD in Social Welfare from Yeshiva University and a Master of Social Work from New York University. Catherine is also the author of *Ignore It!: How Selectively Looking the Other Way Can Decrease Behavioral Problems and Increase Parenting Satisfaction* (TarcherPerigee, 2017).

Catherine's parenting columns have appeared in CNN, the *Los Angeles Times*, *Sports Illustrated*, *HuffPost*, *The Wall Street Journal*, *U.S. News & World Report*, Fatherly, BuzzFeed, Grown & Flown, *Your Teen* magazine, *Romper*, and *Lifehacker*, and on many parenting websites around the world. She is regularly called upon to provide expert opinion for newspaper and magazine articles, speaking engagements, radio, and television.

Catherine lives in California with her sportswriting husband, Jeff; their two kids; and their puppy, Poppy. For more information on Catherine and her work or to find out how to have her visit your school, check out her website: www.thefamilycoach.com.